Ellington Middle School
Library Media Center

Albert Einstein

and His Theory of Relativity

Ellington Middle School
Library Media Center

by Don Herweck

Science Contributor
Sally Ride Science
Science Consultants
Michael E. Kopecky, Science Educator
Jane Weir, Physicist

MISSION: SCIENCE

Developed with contributions from Sally Ride Science™

Sally Ride Science

Sally Ride Science™ is an innovative content company dedicated to fueling young people's interests in science.

Our publications and programs provide opportunities for students and teachers to explore the captivating world of science—from astrobiology to zoology.

We bring science to life and show young people that science is creative, collaborative, fascinating, and fun.

To learn more, visit www.SallyRideScience.com

First hardcover edition published in 2009 by
Compass Point Books
151 Good Counsel Drive
P.O. Box 669
Mankato, MN 56002-0669

Editor: Mari Bolte
Designer: Heidi Thompson
Editorial Contributor: Sue Vander Hook

Art Director: LuAnn Ascheman-Adams
Creative Director: Joe Ewest
Editorial Director: Nick Healy
Managing Editor: Catherine Neitge

 This book was manufactured with paper containing at least 10 percent post-consumer waste.

Library of Congress Cataloging-in-Publication Data
Herweck, Don.
  Albert Einstein and his theory of relativity / by Don Herweck.
    p. cm. — (Mission: Science)
  Includes index.
  ISBN 978-0-7565-4072-2 (library binding)
  1. Einstein, Albert, 1879-1955—Juvenile literature. 2. Relativity (Physics)—Juvenile literature.
  3. Physicists—Biography—Juvenile literature. I. Title. II. Series.
  QC16.E5H47 2009
  530.092—dc22
  [B]   2008035729

Visit Compass Point Books on the Internet at *www.compasspointbooks.com*
or e-mail your request to *custserv@compasspointbooks.com*

Table of Contents

Albert Einstein is considered to be the most famous and most brilliant scientist of all time. He is known both for his exceptional mind and his gentle spirit. His theories, image, and even his name have become synonymous with "genius."

Einstein had an amazing ability to understand how the universe works. He studied how matter and energy work together to make our world and universe function—a science called physics. Perhaps his best-known accomplishment is his formula—$E=mc^2$. When people think of Einstein, they usually think of this formula. But what does it mean?

$E=mc^2$ is about energy. Einstein concluded that energy (E) is equal to mass (m) multiplied by the speed of light (c) squared (^{2}), or multiplied by itself. The speed of light is about 186,000 miles (300,000 kilometers) per second. That's incredibly fast. According to his formula, if the energy of just one atom were released—its mass multiplied by the speed of light squared—it would produce an incredible amount of energy.

On July 16, 1945, Einstein's formula was proved. Before the sun rose that day, the first atomic bomb exploded in a remote area of New Mexico. It began with a huge burst of light. Then

The Speed of Light

The speed of light is not exactly 186,000 miles (300,000 km) per second. It changes, depending on what's in its way. But if light traveled in a vacuum—space that contains no air or matter—its speed would not change. In a vacuum, the speed of light is exactly 186,282.397 miles (299,792.458 km) per second.

came a deep rumbling roar, and a huge mushroom-shaped cloud rose high into the air. The source of this massive display of energy was tiny atoms, split to release their energy ($E=mc^2$). A chain reaction followed, unleashing a force bigger than anything people had ever known. It could be used for good or for evil.

⬆ Einstein hoped that building the bomb would bring about peace. It was his wish that it would never have to be used.

Top Secret!

Einstein knew about the Manhattan Project, a top-secret plan to produce a nuclear bomb. It had started in 1942. Einstein was troubled by the idea of a bomb. He didn't want his formula to be used to create such a terrible weapon.

Despite his objections, the atomic, or nuclear, bomb was tested and then used to end World War II. U.S. President Harry S. Truman ordered that bombs be dropped on two Japanese cities.

On August 6, 1945, an atomic bomb nicknamed "Little Boy" was dropped on the city of Hiroshima. Three days later, on August 9, "Fat Man" was dropped on the city of Nagasaki. Together the bombs killed about 220,000 people. Japan surrendered five days later.

Albert Einstein was born March 14, 1879, in Ulm, Württemberg, Germany. His parents, Hermann and Pauline Einstein, were Jewish, although they didn't observe the traditional religious practices. In Albert's first year, his family moved to Munich. His father and uncle opened a business there that manufactured electrical parts. At home, Albert's mother filled her son's world with music. At the age of 6, Albert began taking violin lessons. An appreciation for music would stay with him the rest of his life.

Albert didn't talk much when he was little. In fact, some people thought he wasn't smart. He would later prove them very wrong. Even at the age of 5, his thoughts were on how the universe worked. Albert was sick in bed when his father brought him a compass from the shop. Albert imagined a mysterious force behind the compass needle.

Einstein was photographed with his sister Maja in about 1884. He enjoyed physics-related puzzles even when he was a young boy.

He would discover that the needle moved by a force called magnetism. This opened the world of physics to him. Einstein later wrote, "That experience made a deep and lasting impression on me. Something deeper had to be hidden behind things."

Afterward he knew that he wanted to study science. Albert built models and mechanical things for fun. Relatives and friends loaned him math and science books. By the age of 12, he taught himself mathematics.

School bored Albert. Some considered him to be a slow learner because he was always asking questions. But he discovered ways to learn on his own, finding out everything he could from books and from his father's business. Einstein once said, "The only thing that interferes with my learning is my education."

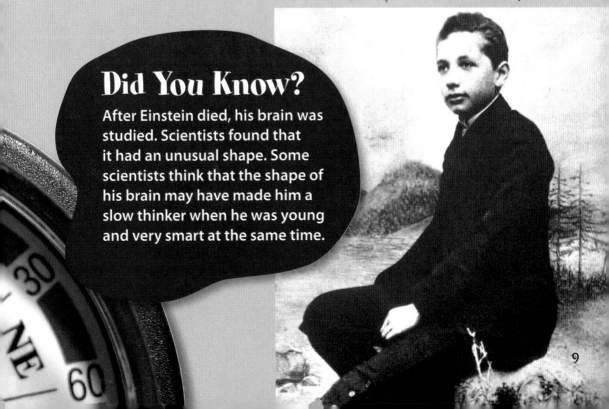

▼ Albert Einstein as a boy

Did You Know?

After Einstein died, his brain was studied. Scientists found that it had an unusual shape. Some scientists think that the shape of his brain may have made him a slow thinker when he was young and very smart at the same time.

When Albert was 15, his family moved to Milan, Italy. Since he only had one more year of high school, Albert stayed behind in Germany to attend school. During his time away from his family, he wrote his first scientific work—a paper on magnetism.

Albert liked to learn, but he strongly disliked the strict German school system. Later he said, "It's a true miracle that modern education hasn't yet completely smothered the curiosity necessary for scientific study."

Before he graduated, Albert left school and joined his family in Milan. He didn't want to be forced to become a German soldier after graduation. In fact, the idea of war frightened and disgusted him. When he was 17, he gave up his German citizenship. That year he enrolled in the Swiss Federal Institute of Technology in Zurich, Switzerland. There he studied physics, a field that would challenge his mind and his imagination. "Imagination is more important than knowledge," he said. "Knowledge is limited. Imagination encircles the world."

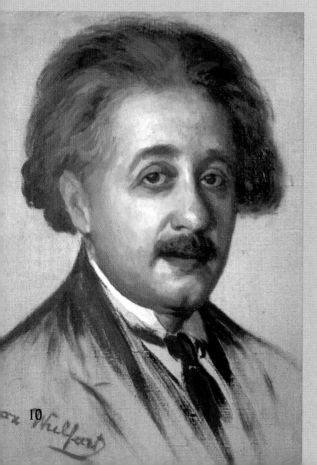

Einstein was so focused on studying that he didn't bother to pay attention to things like combing his hair.

When Einstein graduated four years later, he was qualified to teach. For two years, he taught in various places and did some tutoring. But finally he accepted a position in the Swiss patent office in Bern, Switzerland. He became an assistant technical examiner. This meant he reviewed patent applications from inventors.

Einstein's specialty at the patent office was electromagnetic devices. He knew a lot about them from what he had learned at his father's shop. This made his job easy, which gave him time to think about how the universe works.

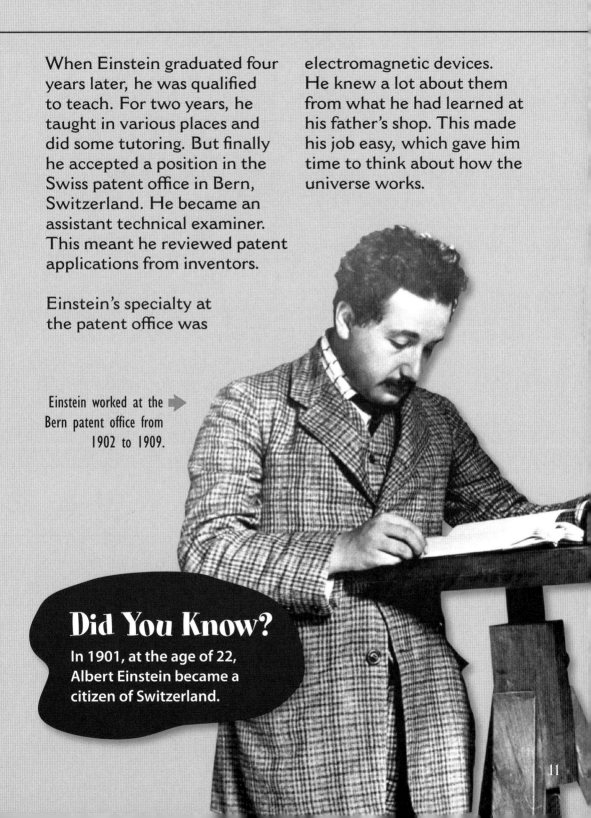

Einstein worked at the Bern patent office from 1902 to 1909.

Did You Know?

In 1901, at the age of 22, Albert Einstein became a citizen of Switzerland.

During his years at the Swiss Federal Institute of Technology, Einstein met and fell in love with a fellow student. Mileva Maric was the only female student studying mathematics at the college. In 1902, they had a daughter together. The following year, on January 6, 1903, Albert and Mileva were married. In 1904, a son, Hans Albert, was born.

In his spare time, Einstein wrote scientific papers filled with new ideas. In 1905 alone, he published four papers in *Annalen der Physik*, an important German physics journal. It was an astounding accomplishment for the 26-year-old patent reviewer. That year would come to be called his *annus mirabilis*—his "miraculous year."

That year, Einstein was awarded an honorary doctorate from the University of Zurich. His doctoral thesis was titled *A New Determination of Molecular Dimensions*. Most scientists didn't consider Einstein's papers very important. Some outright rejected his ideas, and many thought his work was controversial.

But he was becoming famous for his ideas and theories. He would soon be considered by many to

Did You Know?

Three of Einstein's papers were published in the same volume—Volume 17—of the 1905 edition of the scientific journal *Annalen der Physik*. At a 1994 auction, copies of that famous edition of the journal sold for $15,000.

be one of the world's leading scientific thinkers.

Einstein was finding answers to some tough problems that scientists had not been able to solve. He found new ways to look at problems. His papers became the building blocks for physics. Scientists can also use Einstein's solutions to answer their own questions today.

Happy the Way He Was

Einstein was known for being a bit of a slob. He didn't think formal dress was all that important. And he didn't like to wear socks. He said, "When I was young, I found out that the big toe always ends up making a hole in the sock. So, I stopped wearing socks."

◄ Einstein was not a popular student with his teachers. He was known for joking around and cutting class, and his test scores were average at best.

In Einstein's first paper for the *Annalen der Physik*, he gently suggested a new idea about the structure of light. He stated that light is made of tiny particles (now called light photons), and each particle is an independent piece of energy. He called it light quanta. This idea of light quanta was an outrageous claim at that time. It went against the accepted theories of physicists such as Michael Faraday and James Maxwell. They believed that light was a wave that moved about in a substance called ether.

But scientists had noticed something strange about light. When they shined a bright light onto a metal surface, an electric current ran through the metal. They didn't know why this happened. Einstein explained it: Particles in the light hit the electrons in the metal—and released them. Light had caused the metal to give off electricity. It was called the photoelectric effect.

Einstein also showed that the amount of electricity released by the metal depended on the color of the

The Colors of Light

Light from the sun or a lightbulb looks white to you. In fact, it is a combination of many colors. Usually the colors blend together, but sometimes they can be seen individually. The colors are visible when you see a rainbow. The colors of light can also be "split" by using a prism.

The colors in light include red, orange, yellow, green, blue, and violet. Each color has a different wavelength and a different amount of energy. Violet has the shortest wavelength, but it has the most energy. Red, on the other hand, has the longest wavelength but the least energy.

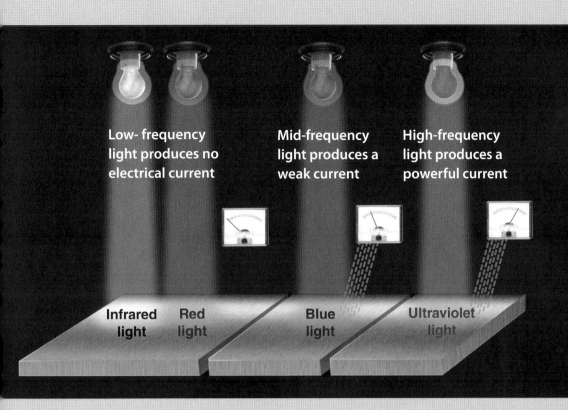

Low- frequency light produces no electrical current

Mid-frequency light produces a weak current

High-frequency light produces a powerful current

Infrared light

Red light

Blue light

Ultraviolet light

light. Einstein's experiments with colored light showed that blue light releases electrons from the metal, but red light does not. He also found that ultraviolet light produces a stronger electrical current than blue light. The more energy in the light, the more electricity the metal released.

Did You Know?

As light travels from the sun to Earth, most of the longer light waves, such as red or yellow, pass straight through the air. But shorter light waves, such as blue, are absorbed by gas molecules, dust, and water. The light waves are scattered all over the sky, making the sky blue.

Seventeen years later, Einstein's work was recognized. He received the 1921 Nobel Prize in physics "for his services to Theoretical Physics, and especially for his discovery of the law of the photoelectric effect."

Brownian Motion and Kinetic Energy

Robert Brown (1773–1858)

In May 1905, Einstein sent another scientific paper to the *Annalen der Physik*. It had only been two months since he sent his paper on the photoelectric effect. Now he had another idea about energy—kinetic energy. Einstein explained that heat is produced by the endless agitated motion of atoms. Scientists had observed the movement of atoms, but they hadn't understood it. Einstein was able to explain it in detail.

When tiny particles such as pollen grains float in water, the invisible atoms in the water hit them and make them move around. Water is made of billions of molecules. When these molecules hit the floating pollen, the grains do a sort of jittery dance. The molecules hit from all directions, making the pollen move about randomly.

This dancing movement of particles in liquid or gas had been observed before. It was named Brownian motion, after Robert Brown, a botanist who studied plants. In 1827, Brown saw pollen grains in water under a microscope. They were moving around, but he didn't know why. Until Einstein explained it, Brownian motion was a mystery.

Did You Know?

The Roman poet and philosopher Lucretius describes the Brownian motion of dust particles in his poem *On the Nature of Things*, written about 50 B.C.

Brownian "Assembly"

The energy produced in Brownian motion can be harnessed, or trapped. Think of a school assembly in the gym. Imagine if everyone moved into one classroom. They would be packed in tightly with little or no room to move. Now imagine putting some huge beach balls in the room. They would stay in place because nothing in the room is in motion. Now what happens if everyone starts moving? The balls are forced to move, too, although not very much because the room is so crowded. As everyone tries to run around the room, some students are forced out the door. Now the balls can move faster and farther because there is more room and more distance between students. The energy in the room makes the temperature rise. This is an example of harnessing the energy produced by Brownian motion. A whole "roomful" of molecules hits objects, energy is released, and the "room" heats up.

With Brownian motion, the large green pollen grains are jostled about by the much smaller water molecules, which are always moving around.

Just a month later, in June 1905, Einstein sent a third paper to the German journal. He was still interested in light, and now he solved yet another mystery. He called his solution the *Special Theory of Relativity*.

At the time, scientists believed that light waves worked like waves in the ocean that travel through water. They thought light waves traveled through a substance called ether. There was one problem, however. When scientists Albert Michelson and Edward Morley tried to measure ether, they couldn't find any.

Einstein explained that light didn't need to travel through anything. He said that light was different from ocean waves. It didn't need anything to push it along. Light always traveled at the same speed, a very high speed. Einstein abbreviated this very large number using the letter C.

Did You Know?

Einstein spoke and read both German and English fluently. But he was a terrible speller. He said he wasn't able to write English because he spelled so poorly.

About Ether

Albert Michelson and Edward Morley weren't trying to disprove ether, but that's what they did. They believed that light has a substance (ether) in which it travels. They conducted an experiment to measure how fast ether carried light. They wanted to find out how ether affected the speed of light.

They thought that if they shined a light in the direction ether was going, the light would go faster. On the other hand, if they shined a light the other way, they expected it to slow down. But no matter which direction they shined the light, the speed of light was always the same. Ether wasn't carrying the light along or slowing it down—because ether didn't exist.

▲ Albert Michelson (1852—1931)

▲ Edward Morley (1838—1923)

The Speed of Light

Einstein had still more ideas about light—especially concerning his discovery that light acts differently from ocean waves. If you were on a ship, you could travel along with the waves. From where you stood on the deck, the waves might look as though they weren't moving. The ship could travel faster than the waves, and then the waves would look as though they were going backwards.

But light works differently. Light always looks as if it is traveling at the same speed—about 186,000 miles (300,000 km) per second, no matter how fast you are traveling. Imagine that you are riding very fast on a bicycle. Your friend is shining a flashlight ahead of you. If you pedal in the same direction the light is shining, no matter how fast you go, the light will still shine ahead as if you were standing still. How could that be? Einstein had the answer.

Light Years

Because light takes time to travel, the farther away the object is, the longer it takes for the image of that object to reach us. The distance is measured in "light" measurements—for example, it takes 1.2 seconds for an image of the moon to reach us on Earth. So we see the moon as it was 1.2 light-seconds ago.

Things that are farther away are measured in light-years, or the distance light will travel in a year, which is about 6 trillion miles

(9.6 trillion kilometers). The closest star system to Earth, Proxima Centauri, is more than four light-years away, which means we see it as it was four years ago. With extremely distant galaxies, we see them as they were billions of years ago. Some scientists project that there may be galaxies that we can't see yet because their light has not had enough time to reach us on Earth. To see some of these galaxies, we would have to travel faster than light—which, according to Einstein's special theory of relativity, is impossible.

Einstein said that the faster you go, the slower time goes. Everything also looks shorter, or scrunched up. At very high speeds, the front of your bike will appear to be shrinking back toward the back of your bike. The more you try to catch the light, the slower time goes, and the shorter your bike appears. We don't notice this in everyday life because it only happens close to the speed of light.

Einstein showed that the old definitions of space and time had to change. Space and time were actually the same thing—not space and time, but rather spacetime. And the faster you go in spacetime, the weirder things get.

Too Much Time

Scientists once believed that time was constant, that it moved along at an unchangeable rate. However, some high-speed experiments have shown that time slows down at higher speeds. Atomic clocks, the most accurate clocks in existence, have been found to run more slowly onboard fast-moving space shuttles than on Earth.

At high speeds, distances and times are distorted to keep the speed of light consistent.

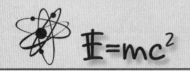

Einstein's fourth paper during his "miraculous year" was written in September 1905. In it he explained the relationship between energy and mass. He wrote his formula as $E=mc^2$. He explained that the energy (E) of an object equals its mass (m) multiplied by the speed of light (c) squared (^{2}).

This means that a very small piece of matter can release an incredible amount of energy. Think about his equation. The speed of light (c) is about 186,000 miles (300,000 km) per second. But we have to multiply 300,000 by itself—and we come up with 90 billion. Then we multiply that huge number by the mass, or weight, of the object. It doesn't matter how little the object is. If you multiply it by 90 billion, it will still be a gigantic number—which translates to a lot of energy.

Einstein didn't write any more papers for a while, but he continued to think and study.

That's a Lot of Energy!

Let's calculate how much energy is in a kilogram (about 35 ounces) of water by using Einstein's formula, $E=mc^2$. A kilogram of water has a little more than 0.111 kg of hydrogen atoms (mass). Now let's multiply 0.111 (m) by the speed of light (c) squared (^{2}).

0.111 kg x (300,000 x 300,000) = 9.99 billion joules

Energy is measured in joules—a unit of energy. One Joule is about the same as the energy released when a dictionary drops to the floor. The hydrogen atoms in a kilogram of water have 9.99 billion joules. That's a staggering amount of energy!

He realized there was something missing from his special theory of relativity. It didn't explain gravity.

The pull of gravity is very strong. It can be felt very far away. For instance, if you were out in space, the gravity of a distant star would pull you toward it before you could even see the star. Einstein wondered if that meant gravity moved faster than light. It would take him 10 years to find the answer.

In 1910, Albert and Mileva's second son, Eduard, was born. In 1911, Einstein moved his family to Prague, where he became a university professor. That same year he attended the world's first physics conference— the Solvay Conference in Brussels, Belgium. Only invited scientists could come. Einstein, then 32 years old, was the youngest physicist there.

Radioactive Research

Shortly before Einstein wrote his paper on $E=mc^2$, scientist Marie Curie was experiencing it. She was working with radium, a radioactive element that gives off a lot of energy. Einstein believed that radium was a perfect example of his formula, constantly changing its mass into energy. Curie also worked with plutonium, another radioactive element. Today the energy made at nuclear power plants comes from radioactive elements that contain a lot of energy. And plutonium is used to power technologies in space such as telecommunication satellites and rovers on Mars.

In 1912, Einstein moved to Switzerland to teach at his old school, the Swiss Federal Institute in Zurich. He also taught physics for a few months at the University of Berlin. But he left a few months before World War I began, in August 1914.

Einstein was still working on his ideas about gravity. He would call his work the general theory of relativity. By 1915, Einstein had concluded that gravity didn't travel faster than light. He discovered that gravity was spacetime

Isaac Newton (1643–1727)

The work of Isaac Newton played an important part in Einstein's theories. Newton was an English mathematician, scientist, and inventor. His three laws of motion are very important in the science of physics. But Einstein's general theory of relativity disproved Newton's theory that space doesn't move or change and that time is the same everywhere.

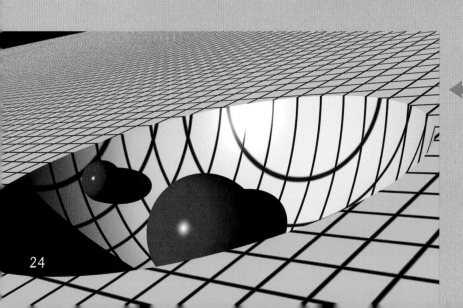

Einstein showed how gravity is the curve of spacetime caused by the mass of stars and planets.

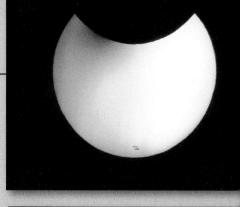

(a combination of space and time) bending around mass and energy. He said that some parts of spacetime bent and curved. The curves were easiest to see around large pieces of mass such as the moon or stars. Planets and other small bodies could fall down the curves or roll around the edges. The objects in space drew other objects toward them.

For more than two centuries, scientists had believed that space was unchanging and that celestial bodies stayed in one spot and always acted the same. Einstein disagreed. His theory about gravity meant that space curved and bent near celestial bodies. In 1919, Einstein's theory of relativity was proved. A solar eclipse allowed scientists to see the stars near the sun. They could see that when the stars passed near the sun, their positions indeed changed.

A solar eclipse in three stages

Did You Know?

Although it is never safe to stare directly at the sun, doing so during a solar eclipse is even more dangerous. The ultraviolet rays from the solar radiation can cause severe eye damage and even loss of vision.

Einstein was awarded science's highest honor in 1922. He received the 1921 Nobel Prize in physics for his work on light quanta.

His personal life had gone through some changes. In 1917, Einstein had been so exhausted that he became seriously ill. His cousin Elsa Löwenthal had taken care of him during his illness. In 1919, Einstein divorced his wife, Mileva, and married Elsa.

Einstein was still pursuing new theories about the universe. In 1927, after his fifth Solvay Conference, he began working on a new idea with Niels Bohr, a Nobel Prize-winning physicist.

In 1932, at the height of his worldwide fame, Einstein was afraid that Germany might make and use an atomic bomb. In 1933, he moved with his wife to Princeton, New Jersey. Three years later, Elsa died after a short illness.

In 1940, Einstein became a U.S. citizen.

Einstein didn't believe in war, but he did believe that action was sometimes needed. In 1939, just after the start of World War II, Einstein sent a letter to U.S. President Franklin Roosevelt. He warned the president that "the element uranium may be turned into a new and important source of energy in the immediate future." He urged the president to build up the country's supply of uranium. The letter led to what was called the Manhattan Project, a U.S. program to build an atomic bomb. The bomb's source of energy was uranium.

Did You Know?

Some of the famous scientists at the 1927 Solvay Conference with Einstein were Niels Bohr, Marie Curie, and Max Planck. Seventeen of the 29 attendees became Nobel Prize winners, including Curie (the only woman), who won twice.

The project began in 1942. But by then Einstein had changed his mind about the bomb. He knew the terrible devastation it could cause. In March 1945, he wrote another letter to the president. Einstein warned Roosevelt not to use the bomb. However, in April, Roosevelt died, and Einstein's letter was later found on the president's desk, unopened.

The next president, Harry Truman, did use the atomic bomb. In August 1945, he ordered that the Japanese cities of Hiroshima and Nagasaki be bombed. More than 220,000 people died from the blasts. Japan surrendered soon after. When Einstein heard the news, he dropped his head in his hands and said, "I could burn my fingers that I wrote that first letter."

Albert Einstein died April 18, 1955, at the age of 76. He is considered the greatest scientist of all time. He gave the world valuable information that is still the foundation for today's discoveries.

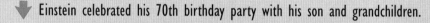
Einstein celebrated his 70th birthday party with his son and grandchildren.

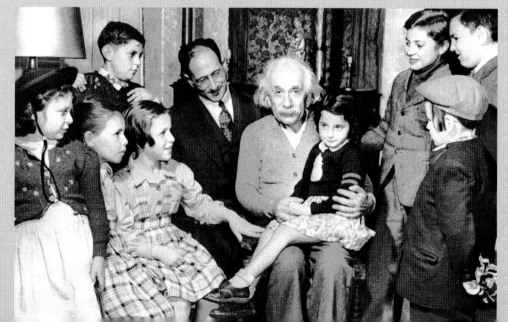

Physicist: Persis Drell

Stanford Linear Accelerator Center

Physicists today use Einstein's theories as a basis for their work. Persis Drell, an American physicist, is best known for what she has discovered about particles, objects that are tinier than an atom. Drell works at the Stanford Linear Accelerator Center in California. There, scientists shoot tiny particles down a tunnel 2 miles (3.2 km) long. The particles travel faster than a speeding bullet and then hit a target at the end. Physicists observe what happens when these particles hit. Sometimes strange new particles are exposed. "I love figuring out what the world is made of at its most basic level," Drell said.

Drell grew up on the Stanford University campus, where her father, Sidney Drell, was a noted physics professor. She didn't like science as a kid, and she even detested physics class in high school. But in college, some great teachers changed her mind. She went on to receive her doctorate in atomic physics from the University of California at Berkeley in 1983. Then she began studying particle physics.

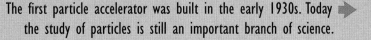

The first particle accelerator was built in the early 1930s. Today the study of particles is still an important branch of science.

Drell now studies very small particles in space. A recent project involved a satellite built to collect space particles. "I've never done anything like that before," she said. "But what I enjoy the most is when I don't know what I'm doing and have to figure it out."

One of Drell's projects still under development is a $6.6 billion international particle accelerator. Scientists from more than two dozen countries are working together on its design. It will smash subatomic particles to expose even smaller particles. This will provide more answers to questions about how the universe works.

Particle collision occurs when two beams of particles are shot directly at each other.

Life and Work at a Glance

Name:	Albert Einstein (March 14, 1879–April 18, 1955)
Nationality:	German; German-Swiss; renounced German citizenship and became an American citizen
Birthplace:	Ulm, Württemberg, Germany
Parents:	Hermann and Pauline (Koch) Einstein
Spouses:	Mileva Maric; Elsa Löwenthal
Children:	Lieserl Einstein (daughter) (1902–?) Hans Albert Einstein (1904–1973) Eduard Einstein (1910–1965)
Place of burial:	Princeton, New Jersey
Field of study:	Physics
Known for:	Photoelectric effect; Brownian motion; special relativity; general relativity; mass-energy equivalence ($E=mc^2$)
Contributions to science:	General relativity; special relativity; Brownian motion; photoelectric effect; mass-energy equivalence ($E=mc^2$); Einstein field equations; unified field theory; Bose-Einstein statistics; EPR paradox
Awards and honors:	Honorary doctorates in science, medicine, and philosophy; Nobel Prize in physics, 1921; Copley Medal (Royal Society of London), 1925; Max Planck Medal, 1929
Publications:	*On a Heuristic Viewpoint Concerning the Production and Transformation of Light*, 1905; *On the Motion—Required by the Molecular Kinetic Theory of Heat—of Small Particles Suspended in a Stationary Liquid*, 1905; *On the Electrodynamics of Moving Bodies*, 1905; *Does the Inertia of a Body Depend Upon Its Energy Content?* 1905; *The Field Equations of Gravitation*, 1915; *Cosmological Considerations in the General Theory of Relativity*, 1917

1879	Albert Einstein is born March 14
1884	Receives his first compass, inspiring him to investigate the mysteries of Earth and the universe
1894	Family moves to Italy but he stays in Munich to finish school; a few months later he leaves school and follows his family to Italy
1896	Graduates from high school at the age of 17; enrolls at the Federal Polytechnic School in Zurich, Switzerland
1900	Graduates from the Federal Polytechnic School
1901	Becomes a citizen of Switzerland; searches for work as a teacher
1902	Has a daughter with Mileva Maric, whom he met at school
1903	Marries Mileva Maric
1904	First son, Hans Albert, is born
1905	His famous "miracle year"; publishes scientific papers in prestigious German journal; one paper develops his special theory of relativity; another paper outlines his formula $E=mc^2$
1907	Begins to apply the laws of gravity to his special theory of relativity
1910	Second son, Eduard, is born
1911	Moves with his family to Prague, in what is now the Czech Republic, to become a professor at the German University; attends Solvay Conference in Brussels, the world's first physics conference; at 32, he is the youngest physicist in attendance

1912	Moves with his family to Zurich to become a professor of theoretical physics at the Federal Polytechnic School
1914	Lives briefly in Berlin, Germany, but returns to Zurich several months before World War I begins
1915	Publishes his general theory of relativity
1919	Divorces his wife, Mileva, and marries his cousin Elsa Löwenthal
1922	Awarded the 1921 Nobel Prize in physics
1927	Attends the fifth Solvay Conference; works with Niels Bohr to develop quantum mechanics
1933	Moves to Princeton, New Jersey; becomes a professor at the Institute for Advanced Study
1936	Wife Elsa dies
1939	Sends letter to U.S. President Franklin Roosevelt urging the United States to build an atomic bomb before Germany does
1940	Becomes an American citizen
1949	Ex-wife, Mileva, dies
1955	Dies of heart failure April 18

Glossary

atomic bomb—bomb created by breaking apart an atom, exerting devastating force

Brownian motion—theory that explains how small particles like molecules move

electromagnetic—state in which magnetism has been produced by an electric charge in motion

electron—particle that has a negative charge of electricity and travels around the nucleus of an atom

energy—power to do work

general theory of relativity—Einstein's theory that explains the effect of gravity on the shape of space and the flow of time

joule—very small unit of energy

light photon—energy packets in light

light wave—visible electromagnetic radiation; the transfer of energy by regular vibration

magnetism—natural force that creates attraction

mass—physical amount of a solid body; bulk or volume

molecule—smallest part of a compound that still retains the compound's properties

patent—right to be the only one to make, use, or sell an invention for a certain number of years

photoelectric effect—giving off of free electrons from a metal surface when light strikes it

physicist—specialist in physics, the science of force and motion

plutonium—radioactive element used in nuclear power plants and to make nuclear weapons

quanta—particles of an atom, now called photons

radium—highly radioactive element found in pitchblende, a blackish mineral

spacetime—dimension consisting of both space and time to identify the location and timing of an object or event

special theory of relativity—Einstein's theory that explains the motion of particles near the speed of light

ultraviolet light—located beyond the visible spectrum at its violet end and having a wavelength shorter than that of visible light but longer than those of X-rays

uranium—heavy, radioactive element often used for nuclear fuels and nuclear weapons

André Marie Ampère (1911–1988)
French physicist and mathematician who laid the
foundation of the science of electrodynamics and
determined that electric currents produce magnetic fields

Antoine Henri Becquerel (1852–1908)
French physicist who discovered radioactivity by
accident in 1896 when a piece of uranium left in a dark
desk drawer made an image on photographic plates

Niels Bohr (1885–1962)
Danish physicist who received the Nobel Prize in
physics in 1922 for his contribution to understanding
the structure of atoms that are made up of protons,
neutrons, and electrons

Max Born (1882–1970)
German-born British physicist known for his work on
the probability interpretation of quantum mechanics

Irène Joliot-Curie (1897–1956)
French chemist and daughter of Marie and Pierre
Curie, who together with her husband received the
Nobel Prize in chemistry in 1935 for the discovery of
artificial radioactivity

Marie Sklodowska-Curie (1867–1934)
Polish/French physicist and chemist who was awarded
two Nobel Prizes (1903 and 1911) for her pioneering
work in radioactivity

Pierre Curie (1859–1906)
French physicist who shared the Nobel Prize with his
wife, Marie Curie, in 1903 for their research on radiation

John Dalton (1766–1844)
English chemist and physicist best known for developing
the atomic theory

Michael Faraday (1791–1867)
British physicist and chemist who proposed the idea of magnetic "lines of force," developed the first electric generator, and pioneered the study of low temperatures

Werner Heisenberg (1901–1976)
German physicist who developed the uncertainty principle, which advanced modern physics; realized that the atomic nucleus consisted of protons and neutrons; won the Nobel Prize in 1932

James Joule (1818–1889)
British physicist who determined the amount of heat produced by an electric current (named joule in his honor); determined that if a gas expands without performing work, its temperature falls

Ernst Mach (1838–1916)
Austrian physicist who discovered that airflow becomes disturbed at the speed of sound; mach numbers, which represent how fast a craft is traveling beyond the speed of sound, were named after him

James Maxwell (1831–1879)
British physicist who developed equations that served as a basis for the understanding of electromagnetism; determined that light is electromagnetic radiation and predicted other types of radiation beyond visible light; developed the kinetic theory of gases, a foundation of modern physical chemistry

Maria Goeppert-Mayer (1906–1972)
American physicist known for her research on the nucleus of an atom; received the Nobel Prize in physics in 1963, becoming the second woman to receive the award (Marie Curie was the first)

Dimitri Ivanovich Mendeleev (1834–1907)
Russian chemist credited with creating the first version of the periodic table of the elements

Albert Michelson (1852–1931)

American physicist who accurately determined the speed of light, accurate to within several thousandths of a percent; with Edward Morley, he invented the interferometer to show that light travels at a constant velocity, regardless of the movement of Earth, an idea that eventually led to Einstein's theory of relativity

Edward Morley (1838–1923)

American chemist and physicist who, along with Albert Michelson, developed the interferometer to show that the velocity of light is a constant (called the Michelson-Morley experiment)

Isaac Newton (1643–1727)

English physicist and mathematician who was one of the greatest scientists of all time; invented calculus, determined the nature of white light, constructed the first reflecting telescope, and formulated the laws of motion and the theory of universal gravitation

Julius Oppenheimer (1904–1967)

American physicist who, along with his work in astrophysics, was the director of the Manhattan Project to build the first atomic bomb

Max Planck (1858–1947)

German physicist who used the quantum theory to explain the nature of black-body radiation, where energy is discontinuous; awarded the Nobel Prize in 1918

Ernest Rutherford (1871–1937)

English physicist who studied the element uranium and became known as the father of nuclear physics

Joseph John Thomson (1856–1940)

English physicist known for the plum pudding model for an atom's structure and the discoveries of the electron and isotopes; received the Nobel Prize in physics in 1906

Brallier, Jess M. *Who Was Albert Einstein?* New York: Grosset & Dunlap, 2002.

Delano, Marfe Ferguson. *Genius: A Photobiography of Albert Einstein*. Washington, D.C.: National Geographic Society, 2005.

Fortey, Jacqueline. *Great Scientists*. New York: DK Publishers, 2007.

Solway, Andrew. *A History of Super Science*. Chicago: Raintree, 2006.

Whiting, Jim. *John Dalton and the Atomic Theory*. Hockessin, Del.: Mitchell Lane Publishers, 2005.

On the Web

For more information on this topic, use FactHound.

1. Go to *www.facthound.com*
2. Choose your grade level.
3. Begin your search.

This book's ID number is 9780756540722

FactHound will find the best sites for you.

Index

Don Herweck

Don Herweck was born and educated in southern California and has degrees in math, physics, and physical science. Currently he is an operations manager for a large automotive manufacturer and travels internationally and throughout the United States for his business. He is the father of four children and has recently returned to California after several years living in the South and Midwest.

Image Credits